This belongs to: _____

MW00380874

Around
the
TABLE

Workshop Handbook

Copyright © 2019 Leah's Pantry (leahspantry.org).

Founded in 2006, Leah's Pantry has expanded from providing innovative nutrition education programming for low-income populations in San Francisco to a statewide organization that works with public and private partners. In addition to our grassroots work, we work throughout California to conduct nutrition educator training, manage the EatFresh.org website, and provide a comprehensive training and capacity building program for charitable food pantries. We are the first nutrition organization in the country to adopt a trauma-informed approach.

All rights reserved. No part of this publication may be reproduced, distributed, or transmitted in any form or by any means, outside of the Partnership Agreement between Leah's Pantry and partner organizations using **Around the Table** curriculum.

Funded by USDA SNAP, an equal opportunity provider and employer.

ISBN: 9781091081376

Printed by Amazon KDP in the United States of America. Some images sourced from Unsplash and Adobe Stock.

v.04052019

Welcome to Around the Table!

What does food mean to you? How do you connect to the food you eat and the people you eat with? Do you like to cook or want to improve your cooking skills? Are you nervous about cooking for yourself or just interested in learning how to prepare new recipes? Do you ever think about how to best nourish your body and your mind? Do you want to learn new ways of taking care of yourself?

You are invited to gather with your community to spend time cooking, sharing, and exploring these things together. *Enjoy!*

Contents

■ Food and Cooking Skills 7

    Kitchen Safety.. 8

    Knife Skills... 9

    Cuts to Know 10

    How to Follow a Recipe... 11

    How to Measure 12

    Don't Label Me!.. 14

    Outsmart the Grocery Store.. 15

    Canned, Boxed, and Bagged... 16

■ Nourishing Myself 17

    Soup Bowl Breathing... 18

    5-4-3-2-1... 19

    Meaning of Food in Life: What Motivates your Food Choices? 20

    Food, Mood, and Energy 22

    Mindful Eating 24

    Your Healthiest, Happiest Self.. 25

    Table Talk Questions... 26

■ Menu Planning... 27

    Menus.. 28

    Meal Planner & Budget Tracker.. 31

■ Recipes 33

    Baby Tomato Bites 34

    Banana Sushi... 35

    Black Bean and Vegetable Tostada... 36

    Chicken Caesar Pasta Salad.. 37

    Chicken Lettuce Wraps... 38

    Chicken Soft Tacos.. 39

    Corn and Black Bean Salad... 40

    Egg Burritos.. 41

    Fish Tacos 42

    Fresh Veggies and Dip 43

Fruit Crisp 44

Fudgy Fruit 45

Green Smoothie 46

Korean-Style Vegetable Pancakes 47

Meatball Soup 48

Mu Shu Vegetables 49

No-cook Chocolate Pudding 50

Pear, Grape, and Cucumber Salad 51

Pita Pizza 52

Popcorn and Toppings 53

Salsa Fresca 54

Sautéed Bananas 55

Sesame Chicken Stir-Fry 56

Spaghetti with Meat Sauce 57

Spiced Trail Mix 58

Spinach and Citrus Salad 59

Spring Spread 60

Three Bean Chili 61

Turkey Apple Sausage Muffin Sandwiches 62

Un-Fried Rice 63

Vegetable Noodle Bowl 64

Vegetarian Sushi Roll 65

Veggie Scramble 66

Whole Wheat Pancake 67

Yogurt Parfait 68

Write Your Own Recipe: Oven-baked Omelette (a.k.a. Frittata) 69

Write your Own Recipe: Cheesy Baked Pasta 70

Write Your Own Recipe: Dinner Salad 71

Write your Own Recipe: Fried "Rice" 72

Recipe Template 73

EatFresh.org 74

■ **Survey** **75**

FOOD AND COOKING SKILLS

KITCHEN SAFETY

 How do you practice safe cooking in the kitchen?
Consider these guidelines.

☑ *Prevent burns*

- » Put foods gently into boiling water so it will not splash.
- » Lift lids from hot pots with the opening away from you.
- » Do not put hot grease into water or add water to hot grease, as it will splatter.
- » Turn the handles of pots and pans inward.
- » Food heated in the microwave has hot and cold spots. Always stir it before eating.
- » Use a dry potholder or oven mitt when handling pots and pans from the oven, stove, or microwave.
- » Keep wet hands away from electrical outlets.

☑ *Prevent fires*

- » Tie back hair and avoid wearing loose clothing or jewelry that could touch the burner or flame.
- » Keep dish towels, potholders, and printed recipes away from hot burners.
- » Use microwave-safe cookware; avoid microwaving in plastic, especially if not labeled microwave-safe.
- » Metal will make sparks in a microwave, so don't put the following into your microwave: food inside a stapled bag, tin foil, forks, or knives.
- » Don't leave food unattended in a microwave or on the stove.
- » Know where your fire extinguisher is and how to use it.

☑ *Prevent illness*

- » Wash your hands with soap and warm water before handling food and after handing raw meat or poultry. Wash all utensils and other materials after they have touched raw meat, before using them with other ingredients.
- » Don't leave cooked food at room temperature for more than two hours.

👍 *Consider these five rules for safe knife care. Refer to the images for the best way to hold your knife.*

» **Let it fall.** Never try to catch a falling knife (and always wear closed-toe shoes in the kitchen).

» **Keep away.** If you need to walk away from the cutting board, put your knife alongside the top edge of the cutting board. Store knives in a block or wrapped in a towel in a drawer.

» **"Knife behind you."** If you must leave the table with a knife, carry it safely by your side with the tip down and the sharp edge facing back. Let others who are near you know you are walking with a knife by announcing "knife behind you."

» **Hand wash.** Never put a knife in a sink full of water or dishes. Wash by hand and dry well before putting it away.

» **Clean in between.** Clean your knife between food items, especially between ready to eat items and raw ingredients. Also, use a clean cutting board.

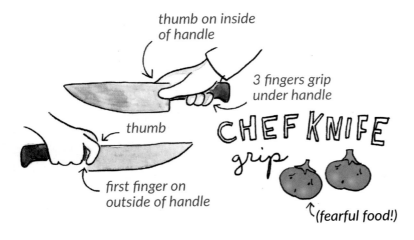

thumb on inside of handle

3 fingers grip under handle

thumb

first finger on outside of handle

CHEF KNIFE grip

(fearful food!)

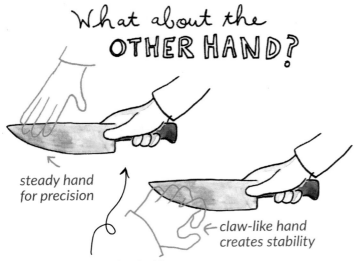

What about the OTHER HAND?

steady hand for precision

claw-like hand creates stability

Pinch the blade of the knife for a stronger grip and more control over the knife.

Cutting an Onion

1 Cut in half lengthwise, from the root to the tip. If you want something to hold onto while dicing, cut off the stem tip but not the root.

2 Peel away the skin. Washing it in cold water can help release the skin and also lessen the odor.

3 Cut in half widthwise.

4 Slice lengthwise.

5 Chop widthwise.

FOOD AND COOKING SKILLS

Use the claw (fingertips and thumb tucked under) to hold the food you are cutting to protect yourself from cuts.

Cut fruit or vegetable in half to create a flat surface to make it easier to control. Round things then can't roll away.

Always use a sharp knife.

↑ Slice

Place a damp towel under the cutting board to avoid slippage.

Dice ↓

↑ Julienne

Angle/bias ↓

When cutting something make sure the knife is moving towards the cutting board using either a push cut or pull cut.

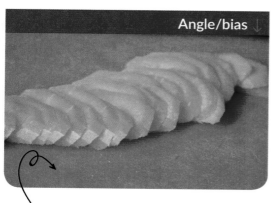

Mince ↓

Choose a knife and cutting board that are large enough and appropriate for the job that you are doing.

↓ Chiffonade

Use the back of the knife to scrape or transfer food off of your cutting board.

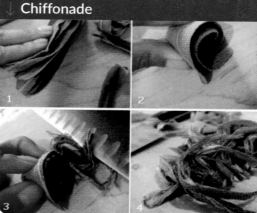

Always look at what you are doing.

FOOD AND COOKING SKILLS

👍 *First, read the recipe all the way through.* Then, grab a pen or pencil and read it again, while taking notes to answer these questions. Continue to take notes as you cook, to make it easier the next time you prepare the recipe.

1 Are there any terms or measurements you don't know or understand?

2 Do you need to double the recipe or cut it in half?

visit **eatFresh**.org · Tasty Recipes On Your Budget · 📱 🖥 #eatfreshCA

| Ready In 30 min. | Serves 4 |

Whole Wheat Pancakes

Ingredients

- 1 cup <u>whole wheat</u> flour
- 2 teaspoons baking powder
- ¼ teaspoon salt
- 1 egg
- 1 cup milk or non-dairy alternative

- 1 tablespoon canola oil or melted butter (optional)
- 1 cup chopped ripe banana, thin-sliced apple, or frozen blueberries (optional)
- oil or butter *for greasing pan*

Directions

1. Put oil or butter in skillet; heat for a moment on medium-low.
2. In a bowl, mix together dry ingredients. Whisk in eggs and milk, then stir in 1 tbsp. melted butter or oil, if using.
3. Spoon 1/4 cup batter into the hot skillet.
4. Once pancake is bubbling and dry around the edges, flip it. ✳
5. Cook about 3 minutes more, until the center is completely dry. Remove from pan. Repeat until batter is finished.

This recipe can also be made in a rice cooker: Pour all of the batter into a greased rice cooker. Cook for 1-2 cycles, until the cake is dry in the middle. Remove dish from cooker and flip pancake onto a plate. (The pancake should pop out.) Slice into 4 and serve.

Nutrition Information *per serving:*
Calories 217 Carbohydrates 34g Fiber 5g Protein 8g Total Fat 7g Sat. Fat 2g Sodium 293mg

Source: Leah's Pantry

Funded by USDA SNAP, an equal opportunity provider and employer.

3 How long will it take to make this?

Prepping and chopping time: _____

Cooking/baking time: _____

Chilling, cooling, or resting time: _____

4 What are the ingredients you need?

5 What is the equipment you need?

6 What is the first thing you will do? (Remember it might not be the first thing listed. Maybe you need to preheat the oven or chop some ingredients, for example.) What is the second thing you will do?

FOOD AND COOKING SKILLS

👍 *Do you know common measurement abbreviations, tools, and equivalents?*

These are helpful in reading and understanding recipes.

☑ *Recognize the abbreviations*

- » Cup: c.
- » Fluid ounce: fl oz.
- » Gallon: g or gal.
- » Gram: g.
- » Kilogram: kg.
- » Milliliter: ml.
- » Ounce: oz.
- » Pound: lb.
- » Quart: q or qt.
- » Teaspoon: t or tsp.
- » Tablespoon: T or tbsp.

☑ *Choose the correct tool*

- » Use measuring spoons for small amounts of liquid or dry ingredients.
- » Use liquid measuring cups for larger amounts of liquids.
- » Use dry measuring cups for larger amounts of solid or semisolid ingredients like flour, rice, or sugar.
- » Recipes sometime give amounts in weight. Non-liquid packaged products sometimes show how much they weigh on the label.
- » Don't confuse liquid ounces with dry ounces.

☑ *Measure accurate equivalents*

- » 3 tsp = 1 tbsp
- » 4 tbsp = 1/4 cup
- » 8 tbsp = 1/2 cup
- » 16 tbsp = 1 cup
- » 4 cups = 1 quart
- » 4 quarts = 1 gallon
- » 1 pound = 16 ounces (dry weight)
- » 1 cup = 8 ounces (liquids only)

Measuring Dry Ingredients

1 Scoop the ingredient into the dry measuring cup or spoon.

2 Use the back of a utensil to smooth the top.

Measuring Liquid Ingredients

1 Fill the liquid measuring cup up to the line.

2 Place it on a level surface to confirm measurement.

3 Bend down so you are at eye-level with the measurement to read it accurately.

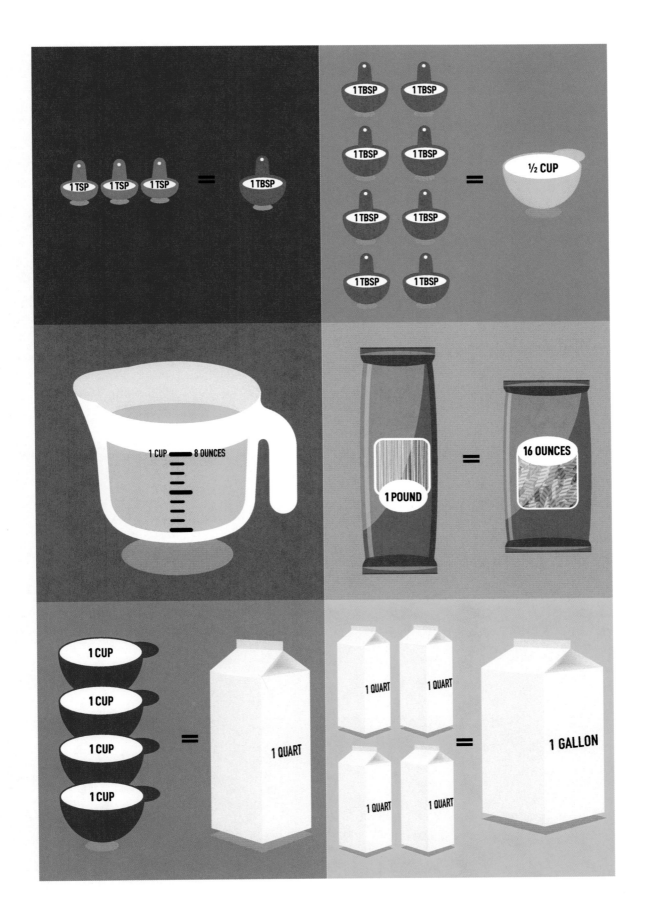

How do you think the design or wording on the front of the package tries to influence you to buy it? Do you look at labels on food packages when you are shopping? What do you usually look for? What one item is most useful for you to look at?

☑ *Use this glossary to explore terms typically found on a food label.*

1. **calories**—the energy provided by a food. *Eating more calories than your body uses leads to weight gain.*

2. **carbohydrate**—a nutrient with calories. This is the body's main source of energy. *Carbohydrate-containing foods with fiber provide longer lasting energy.*

3. **fat**—a nutrient that gives a concentrated form of energy, helps absorb other nutrients, and helps build/repair many parts of the body. *High fat foods are also high in calories. Foods labeled low-fat, reduced-fat, or fat-free may have added sugars or other ingredients to make up for the loss of texture or flavor.*

4. **fiber**—a form of carbohydrate that carries water and waste through the body. *Fiber helps you feel full longer, helps lower cholesterol, and controls blood sugar levels.*

5. **GMO-free**—a food without ingredients that had its genetic material artificially manipulated to produce genetically modified organisms. *Some people choose non-GMO foods out of concern for possible unknown effects on the earth and human health.*

6. **gluten-free**—foods without gluten, a type of protein found in some grains (especially wheat). *Some people cannot digest gluten properly or are allergic.*

7. **organic**—foods grown and processed without the use of chemicals. *People may choose organic foods to avoid chemicals for themselves, or to protect farm workers and the earth from chemicals.*

8. **protein**—a nutrient that forms the building blocks of cells, muscles, and tissues. *In addition to animal foods, many plant foods also contain protein.*

9. **sodium, a.k.a. "salt"**—a mineral the body needs in small amounts. *Too much is unhealthy for people with high blood pressure. Processed foods often have a lot.*

10. **sugars**—a form of carbohydrate that gives instant energy. *Processed foods may have unhealthy amounts of added sugars.*

11. **vegan**—foods without any animal products (including eggs or dairy) and made without harming animals.

12. **vitamins and minerals**—compounds the brain and body need in small amounts to function well. *Whole foods and minimally-processed foods contain more vitamins and minerals.*

13. **whole grains**—grains that have not had anything removed in processing. *These have more vitamins, minerals, and fiber than "refined" white grains like white flour and white rice.*

How does the layout of your grocery store shape your choices?
Where are the healthiest foods are located?
Are products displayed at the ends of aisles always on sale?
Why are candy and magazines always near the register?
What types of food do you think make the store a higher profit?

TIPS

☑ **Make a plan, come with a list.** Planning your meals ahead of time and using a shopping list saves time, saves money, and encourages healthier eating.

32 OZ LF YOGURT		6 OZ LF YOGURT	
UNIT PRICE **$0.05** per oz	RETAIL PRICE **$1.62**	UNIT PRICE **$0.12** per oz	RETAIL PRICE **$0.72**
8465197255548123		8465197846665559	

☑ **Compare unit prices.** Unit prices allow you to compare the price of two packages that may contain a different amount of food. Larger packages often have lower unit prices; however, be sure to consider whether you'll be able to eat the entire amount before it goes bad.

☑ **Look up and look down.** The most expensive or profitable products are often placed right at eye level. Look on the higher and lower shelves to see if there are cheaper alternatives. Also, watch out for special displays at the end of the aisle. That doesn't mean it's on sale. Sometimes it's just there to get you to buy it.

☑ **Compare brands.** Store brands and generic products are often identical to name brand products in everything but price. Look at the ingredients list to compare.

☑ **Coupons and sales can be worth it... sometimes.** Coupons and specials can be a good way to save money—when you use them wisely. Stick to buying bargain items that are already on your list.

☑ **Don't pay for empty calories and low quality ingredients.** Processed foods often contain ingredients that don't cost the manufacturer a lot of money but they can make a big profit from it. A lot of junk food masquerades as healthy with meaningless front-of-packaging labels like "natural." Remember to check the labels.

CANNED, BOXED, AND BAGGED

 Do you know how to make healthy choices regarding packaged foods?

❶ Can you tell what plant or animal it came from?

Choose foods made from ingredients you can picture in their raw state or growing in nature. If you see something you can't pronounce and think it was made in a lab, beware.

❷ Don't be fooled by big health claims or slogans on a package.

They can distract you from something less healthy, such as high sodium or sugar content.

❸ Avoid foods with sugar listed in the first three ingredients.

Also, look for "added sugars" on the nutrition facts label. Be aware that sugar can have a variety of names. Look at the list for some examples. ➤

❹ Look for 100% whole grain foods.

Look for the whole grain label or the word "whole" in the first ingredient. Examples include: whole wheat, whole oats, whole grain corn, and brown rice.

WORDS FOR SUGAR

- » Honey
- » Brown sugar
- » Dextrose
- » Sucrose
- » High fructose corn syrup
- » Fruit juice concentrate
- » Barley malt
- » Cane juice
- » Molasses
- » Brown rice syrup
- » Glucose
- » Caramel

NOURISHING MYSELF

SOUP BOWL BREATHING

When you need to clear your mind, de-stress, get focused, or wind down, try this 90 second exercise.

Think of your favorite soup.

Gently cup your hands like you are holding your favorite soup. You can also just put your hands down in your lap. Sit up tall, like your spine was made of a stack of pennies, with both feet on the floor. Close your eyes or glance down.

Imagine breathing in like you are smelling a delicious bowl of soup, and breathing out like you are blowing on it to cool down—carefully so as not to splash soup everywhere!

Breathe in for four seconds.

Breathe out for eight seconds.

Repeat three times.

Repeat three more times.

Do you need a ritual to connect with your mind, body, or spirit?
Try this one whenever you need it.

Put your feet flat on the ground.

Silently, to yourself, name **five things you can see** in the room...

Now name **four things you can hear** in the room...

Next, name **three sensations you feel in your body**...

Then, name **two things you can smell**...

And finally, [*pick one thing to consider from the list below*]

> ...one thing for which you are grateful.
>
> ...one thing that inspires you.
>
> ...one person you appreciate.
>
> ...one wish for the world.
>
> ...one hope or dream for yourself.
>
> ...one good quality about yourself.

MEANING OF FOOD IN LIFE: WHAT MOTIVATES YOUR FOOD CHOICES?

Have you ever thought about what is important to you about food?
Is it something that is important to your life? In what way?
What values motivate your food choices the most? Moral, social, sacred, aesthetic, or health?
What are some examples of these values in your life?

☑ *Read each statement and rate it on a scale of 1 to 7.*
Add up the totals in each section and divide in order to get your personal rating for each set of values.

1 = I strongly disagree
2 = I mostly disagree
3 = I disagree somewhat
4 = I don't agree or disagree
5 = I agree somewhat
6 = I mostly agree
7 = I strongly agree

MORAL

I care about the impact of my food choice on the world.

My food choices are an important way that I can affect the world.

When I eat food, I think about where it came from.

I eat in a way that expresses care for the world.

My food choices reflect my connection to nature.

÷ 5 =

> *...the degree to which you are concerned with doing the right thing for society, animals, or the environment, when it comes to food.*

SOCIAL

☐	Food is closely tied to my relationships with others.
☐	When I eat, I feel connected to the people I am eating with.
☐	Food is a way for me to connect with my cultural traditions.
☐	Sharing food with others makes me feel closer to them.
☐	Making food for others is a main way I show care for them.
☐	÷ 5 = ☐

...how important interacting and connecting with others around food is to you.

SACRED

☐	What I eat is a reflection of my spiritual beliefs.
☐	From a spiritual perspective, some foods are better than others.
☐	My food choices are a way for me to connect with the sacred.
☐	Some foods are spiritually polluting.
☐	÷ 4 = ☐

...the extent to which your spiritual beliefs and sense of a higher purpose is reflected in how you eat.

AESTHETIC

☐	Preparing a good meal is like making a work of art.
☐	A good meal is like a work of art.
☐	I can appreciate the beauty of a dish even if I do not like it.
☐	Eating a good meal is an aesthetic experience like going to a good concert or reading a good novel.
☐	÷ 4 = ☐

...how much you appreciate the artistry and beauty of good food and the dining experience.

HEALTH

☐	Eating foods that I know are good for my body brings me comfort.
☐	I feel that nourishing my body is a meaningful activity.
☐	I eat in a way that expresses care for my body.
☐	I get satisfaction from knowing that the food I eat is good for my health.
☐	÷ 4 = ☐

...the degree to which you care about having good nourishment to ensure your physical well-being.

Arbit, N., Ruby, M., and Rozin, P., (July 2017). The Meaning of Food in Life Scale: Evidence for Links with Healthy Eating, A Positive Relationship to Food, and Established Determinants of Healthy Eating Behavior. http://www.jneb.org/article/S1499-4046(17)30288-9/pdf

Did you know? A good balanced diet is like building a fire with logs instead of sticks—your fire will burn bigger and longer.

Many people crave **sugar**, **caffeine**, or **highly processed snacks** when tired or "down." These provide quick energy. But they can also cause a crash when the energy wears off, ultimately making energy or mood even worse. Or they may skip meals when anxious, tired, or in a hurry. This can also cause mood or energy crashes and lead to overeating unhealthy food later.

☑ *Improve your mood and energy with good food.*

A diet rich in **healthy fats** and **fiber**, such as found in whole grains, nuts, and seeds, helps you stay full for hours so your energy doesn't crash. **Protein** fills you up and provides amino acids needed for steady moods.

Vitamins and **minerals** from colorful fruits and vegetables can help the body stay strong and adapt to stress. For example:

» **Vitamins A** and **C** are found in many red and orange fruits and vegetables. They protect you from illness as well as fight inflammation (irritation) so your body feels its best.
» **B vitamins** are known as "stress vitamins" because they are so important in helping your body adapt to changes. These are found in dark leafy greens, as well as nuts, seeds, whole grains, and some animal products.

There are many more vitamins and minerals found in fruits and vegetables. That's why doctors recommend: "**Eat a rainbow of fruits and vegetables every day!**"

If you are feeling low energy, unfocused, moody, or agitated, try getting hydrated. **Water** helps to bring nutrients to your muscles so your body can feel more energized. Also, your brain is mostly water, so drinking water can help:

» improve concentration, memory, and learning
» balance your mood and emotions

Eating balanced snacks or meals regularly during your day can keep your energy from plummeting.

☑ *Many of us struggle with keeping up our mood and energy during the day.
What advice would you give to the people below?*

Jasmine tries to be health conscious, but she is very busy and stressed out. She usually eats a light breakfast, such as a bagel, before classes and sometimes buys a soup or salad for lunch. Afterwards, she often buys a large iced mocha for an energy boost to get through her busy afternoon of activities and responsibilities. She is so hungry at the end of the day that she usually eats a large dinner with her family and then snacks on chips or cookies while studying before bed. Sometimes she also has a hard time falling asleep, even after her busy day.

What are some healthy ways Jasmine can better manage her energy to get through the day?

» Carry a healthy snack, like nuts or fruit, and drink water.

» Skip afternoon caffeinated drinks and nighttime sugary treats for a better night's sleep.

» Something else: _____

Nico has to get to his summer job at a grocery store by 8:00 am each morning. He is so cranky and tired in the morning that he doesn't eat breakfast. When he gets to work, he buys a juice or some chips. He is still moody and has a hard time focusing on his job. At lunch he goes out to get his favorite food—cheeseburgers, fries, and a diet coke. Afterwards he feels much better... for a little while. At home he only eats a little dinner and spends the rest of the night in a bad mood again.

What could Nico do to feel better throughout the day?

» Eat something more nourishing for breakfast such as yogurt or whole grain cereal.

» Eat a balanced dinner with fruits and vegetables.

» Something else: _____

MINDFUL EATING

Mindful eating helps us nourish our mind and body.
Use these reminders to help take care of yourself when you eat.

☑ *Learn your hunger cues*—Are you actually hungry or are you instead tired, stressed out, bored, or thirsty?

☑ *Avoid overeating*—Pay attention to your portion size. Slow down as the meal progresses, notice when you are full, and decide if you want to stop eating.

☑ *Pay attention to how you eat*—Take time to taste and enjoy your food. Try not to multitask or use a screen while eating.

☑ *Nourish your mind and body*—Pay attention to what you eat. Food affects how well your mind and body functions.

Imagine that you are your healthiest, happiest self.
What are you doing? Where are you? Who are you with? How does your body feel?

☑ *Write or draw about your healthy, happy self. Create a picture, a simple description, a poem, a song, or whatever you want, but make it about what is important to you.*

TABLE TALK QUESTIONS

 Stir up an interesting conversation with friends and family with these questions. Ask them in the car, at home, at the dining table, over text/chat, on the phone, or anywhere.

1. What is the scariest thing about becoming an adult?

2. What is something you want to learn that they don't teach you in school?

3. Why do you think people give up on their dreams?

4. If you could bring back one person from the dead, who would it be?

5. What is the first step toward ending racism?

6. Why do you think we need to go to school?

7. What is your most important goal right now?

8. What is one lesson that you had to learn the hard way and what did you learn?

9. What are your three best and worst qualities?

10. What do you like most about yourself?

11. If you could teach any class, what would it be?

12. If you could have any talent, what would it be?

13. When do you feel the most protected?

14. Do you believe a person is defined by what he or she does for a living?

15. What is your greatest fear about having children?

16. What makes you angry and how can you change that?

17. What is a piece of wisdom that you would pass on to your kids about being your age?

18. What is your biggest accomplishment and why?

19. If you could change one law, what would it be?

20. What are three traits you look for in a friend?

21. Would you rather have a job with average pay that you love or a job with great pay that you hate?

22. What makes you happy?

23. If you could make any dish in the world, what would you make?

24. Do you consider yourself an optimist or a pessimist?

25. Who is someone that you admire and why?

26. What is an essential life skill you need in order to live on your own?

27. What is a misconception that people have about you?

28. What do you do when you are talking with friends and someone makes an offensive comment (i.e. racist, sexist, homophobic)?

29. Which is more powerful: love or hate?

30. What is one goal you want to achieve in the next year?

31. What is one thing you wish adults understood better about young people and why?

32. What is one thing you wish you understood better about adults and why?

33. If you could meet one historical figure, living or dead, who would it be and why?

34. If you had 5 minutes to meet with the U.S. President, what would you say?

35. What is one thing people don't know about you that you wish they knew?

36. What kind of food best describes your personality?

37. What does health mean to you?

Adapted from: Edible Schoolyard, Question Cards, https://edibleschoolyard.org/resource/sample-question-cards

MENU PLANNING

MENUS

What menu will you prepare?
Consider the following to help you decide.

1. Read every part of the recipe.

2. Can this recipe be prepared in the amount of time available?

3. Can it be prepared with the equipment you have?

4. Does it meet everyone's dietary restrictions?

5. Are there ingredient substitutions that should be made?

6. Are there steps or cooking techniques that should be modified? For example... Buying pre-cooked meat? Using the stove top instead of a slow cooker?

7. Should the number of servings be adjusted?

8. Is the meal balanced, with at least three of the food groups—protein, veggie, fruits, dairy, and grains?

ASIAN-INSPIRED BITES   Choose 1-2.

| Chicken Lettuce Wraps P.38 | Vegetable Noodle Bowl P.64 | Korean-Style Vegetable Pancakes P.47 | Vegetarian Sushi Roll P.65 |

BREAKFAST FOR DINNER   Choose a main dish (left two options) and a side (right two options).

| Egg Burritos P.41 | Turkey Apple Sausage Muffin Sandwiches P.62 | Yogurt Parfait P.68 | Pear Grape Salad P.51 |

QUICK AND HEARTY BREAKFAST Choose 2-3.

Veggie Scramble P.66

Banana Sushi P.35

Spring Spread P.60

Yogurt Parfait P.68

Whole Wheat Pancake P.67

PIZZA OR PASTA PARTY Choose a main dish (left three options) and a dessert (right two options).

Pita Pizza P.52

Chicken Caesar Pasta Salad P.37

Spaghetti with Meat Sauce P.57

No-Cook Chocolate Pudding P.50

Sautéed Bananas P.55

SMOOTHIE AND SNACKS Choose one or more snacks to enjoy with the smoothie.

Green Smoothie P.46

Spiced Trail Mix P.58

Popcorn and Toppings P.53

Fresh Veggies and Dip P.43

Banana Sushi P.35

SOUPS ON!   Choose a main dish (left two options) and a side (right two options).

Meatball Soup P.48   **Three Bean Chili** P.61   **Baby Tomato Bites** P.34   **Spinach and Citrus Salad** P.59

STIR FRY NIGHT   Choose a main dish (left three options) and a dessert (right two options).

Un-Fried Rice P.63   **Mu Shu Vegetables** P.49   **Sesame Chicken Stir-Fry** P.56   **Fruit Crisp** P.44   **Fudgy Fruit** P.45

TACOS TONIGHT   Choose a main dish (left three options) and a side (right two options).

Chicken Soft Tacos P.39   **Fish Tacos** P.42   **Black Bean & Veggie Tostadas** P.30   **Corn and Black Bean Salad** P.40   **Salsa Fresca** P.54

Skip sides if making tostadas.

| MEAL PLAN | SHOPPING LIST | | | | | BUDGETING | |
Recipe/Dish	Produce	Meat	Dairy	Dry, Canned, Boxed	Other	Total Bill	Cost Per Person

MEAL PLAN	SHOPPING LIST					BUDGETING	
Recipe/Dish	Produce	Meat	Dairy	Dry, Canned, Boxed	Other	Total Bill	Cost Per Person

RECIPES

BABY TOMATO BITES

Ready In 15 min.

Serves 6

A healthy snack can be simple and delicious. This easy recipe has only a few ingredients, but it packs a ton of flavor. With ingredients from three food groups, it can also make a light meal.

Ingredients

12 (4-inch) slices of French bread
¼ c. shredded low-fat mozzarella cheese
5 small tomatoes, *diced very small*

½ tsp. black pepper
¼ tsp. salt
8 basil leaves, *chopped*

Directions

1. Preheat oven to 300°F.

2. Place thin layer of mozzarella cheese on each slice of bread.

3. Toast French bread slices in oven until cheese melts, about 5-8 minutes.

4. Mix diced tomatoes, pepper, salt, and basil.

5. Place diced tomatoes on top of toasts. Serve immediately.

Nutrition Info *per 2-slice serving*

Total calories: 190
Carbohydrates: 33 g
Total fat: 3 g
Saturated fat: 1 g
Protein: 9 g
Fiber: 2 g
Sodium: 443 mg

 How would you add even more flavor or nutrients to this recipe?

Do you think this snack is more or less nutritious than other popular snack foods? Why?

How might you make this if you do not have French bread?

Ready In
5 min.

Serves
2

Whole grain bread and tortillas contain more fiber than ones made from white flour. That's why whole grain foods like the tortillas in this recipe may help you stay full for longer. Read ingredients lists to identify whole grain foods; you should see the word "whole" in the first ingredient, for example, "whole wheat flour" or "whole grain oats."

Ingredients

1 8-inch soft whole wheat tortilla
2 tbsp. all-natural peanut butter
Cinnamon to taste

1 banana, *peeled*
1 tbsp. raisins or chopped nuts (optional)

Directions

1. Spread a layer of peanut butter across the tortilla. Leave a gap at the edge about as wide as your fingertip.

2. Sprinkle with raisins or nuts, if using.

3. Shake cinnamon on top of the peanut butter.

4. Place the peeled banana in the middle of the tortilla.

5. Roll the tortilla tightly.

6. Cut into 8 pieces.

✳ *Tip: Try to find a peanut butter with nothing in it but peanuts and salt. Avoid peanut butter with added oil or sugar.*

Nutrition Info *per 4-piece serving*

Total calories: 232
Carbohydrates: 31 g
Total fat: 11 g
Saturated fat: 3 g
Protein: 7 g
Fiber: 5 g
Sodium: 185 mg

How else are whole grain tortillas different from white flour tortillas?

What other fruit or ingredients could you use in this recipe?

What about this snack makes it more filling and provide longer-lasting energy than some other common snacks like chips or muffins?

BLACK BEAN AND VEGETABLE TOSTADA

Ready In 25 min. **Serves** 5

Beans and vegetables on a crispy tortilla combine to be a filling, satisfying, and nourishing meal. It is almost like a fast food taco except you know exactly what you put into it.

Ingredients

1   tbsp. oil, *separated*
¼   c. chopped onion
1   small red bell pepper, *diced*
1   c. canned, defrosted, or fresh corn kernels
1   medium zucchini or yellow squash, *diced*
3   cloves garlic, *finely minced*
1½ c. vegetarian refried black or pinto beans
5   crispy corn tostada shells

4   medium tomatoes, *chopped*
1   small red onion, *chopped*
1   bunch of cilantro, *chopped*
½   cup crumbled Mexican cheese or mild feta

Directions

1.   Heat 2 tsp. oil in medium skillet. Add onion, bell peppers, corn, and zucchini/yellow squash. Cook, stirring occasionally, until vegetables are softened, about 6 minutes. Set aside.

2.   Heat 1 tsp. oil in medium skillet. Add chopped garlic. Cook for 30 seconds. Add can of refried beans. Mix beans and garlic together until smooth and heated through. Set aside.

3.   Spread a thin layer of the bean and garlic mixture on top of a tostada. Add a spoonful of the cooked vegetables. Top the with tomatoes, red onion, cilantro, and cheese.

4.   Eat by picking up the tostada with both hands.

※   *Tip: Make your own tostada shell: Spread out 5 corn tortillas on a foil lined baking sheet. Brush lightly with oil and sprinkle with salt (optional). Bake the tortillas in a preheated 400 degree oven for approximately four minutes per side, or until they are crispy and golden on each side.*

Nutrition Info *per tostada*

Total calories: 233
Carbohydrates: 37 g
Total fat: 8 g
Saturated fat: 2 g
Protein: 8 g
Fiber: 7 g
Sodium: 467 mg
Added Sugar: <1g

 Do you have any friends or family members who might be encouraged to eat vegetables by this recipe?

What other favorite foods could you add fresh vegetables or beans to?

How might you change this recipe if you were in a hurry?

Ready In 25 min. | **Serves** 6

If you find it tough to eat a rainbow of fruits and vegetables every day, then make this salad. A large dinner salad is a good way to eat your veggies when you forgot or didn't have time to during the day.

Ingredients

- 3 c. grilled chicken breast or roasted chicken breast, *chopped or shredded*
- 2 c. dry whole grain penne pasta
- 6 c. Romaine lettuce, *chopped*
- 1½ c. cherry tomatoes halves
- ½ c. fresh basil, *chopped*

- ½ c. green onions, *chopped*
- ¼ c. fresh parsley, *chopped*
- 3 oz. Feta cheese, *crumbled*
- 2 garlic cloves, *minced*
- ⅓ c. Caesar dressing

Directions

1. Cook pasta by following package directions, drain and lightly rinse with cold water.

2. In a large bowl: combine all ingredients and toss until all ingredients are coated with dressing.

3. Serve immediately.

❇ **Tips:** *Experiment with the salad...*
  Substitute the basil/parsley with cilantro
  Substitute the feta cheese for one of your choice
  Try a different type of pasta
  Try it with your favorite dressing
  Try it with sliced olives

Nutrition Info *per ⅙ serving*

Total calories: 346
Carbohydrates: 26 g
Total fat: 14 g
Saturated fat: 4 g
Protein: 29 g
Fiber: 5 g
Sodium: 348 mg

 Which do you think is more satisfying to eat—food with chewy or crunchy texture, or soft, mushy foods? Why?

What other ingredients would you use in this recipe at home? (vegetables, proteins, seasonings)

Can you taste the whole wheat noodles in the recipe, or does the flavor blend in?

CHICKEN LETTUCE WRAPS

Ready In 20 min.

Serves 6

Eating a Rainbow of Fruits and Vegetables is one way to get a variety of vitamins every day. In this easy recipe, ground chicken is mixed with colorful vegetables, cooked, and wrapped in crunchy green lettuce. Using lettuce to wrap cooked meats is a common practice in parts of Asia and makes for a fun and flavorful meal.

Ingredients

1   pound ground chicken
½   onion, *chopped*
Salt and black pepper, *to taste*
2   garlic cloves minced, or 1 tsp. garlic powder
1   inch piece of ginger, *peeled and minced*, or ½ tsp. ginger powder

1   c. celery, *chopped*
1   carrot, *grated*
¼   c. sesame salad dressing or teriyaki sauce
12   large outer lettuce leaves, *rinsed and patted dry*
1   tsp. red chili powder or chili flakes (optional)
¼   c. chopped peanuts (optional)

Stove Top or Skillet Directions

1.   Heat 1 tbsp. oil in the bottom of a skillet.

2.   Add onion and cook for 3 minutes.

3.   Add garlic, ginger, celery, and ground chicken.

4.   Sauté until chicken is cooked through.

5.   Add carrot, dressing or sauce, and optional chili flakes. Cook for 2 more minutes.

6.   Roll about ½ c. of filling into each lettuce leaf like a taco. Sprinkle with optional peanuts.

Microwave Directions

1.   Microwave chicken and onion for 2 minutes.

2.   Stir in garlic, ginger, and celery. Microwave 2-3 more minutes until cooked.

3.   Add carrots, dressing or sauce, and optional chili flakes. Cook for 2 more minutes.

4.   Roll about ½ c. filling in each lettuce leaf like a taco. Sprinkle with optional crushed peanuts.

✳ *Tip: You can make your own teriyaki sauce. Heat 2 tbsp. soy sauce with 1 tbsp. sugar and 1 tbsp. white vinegar in your microwave for about 1 minute. Stir to dissolve the sugar.*

Nutrition Info *per 2-wrap serving*

Total calories: 157   **Total fat:** 10 g   **Protein:** 12 g   **Sodium:** 183 mg
Carbohydrates: 6 g   **Saturated fat:** 2 g   **Fiber:** 2 g

What vegetables could you add to make this dish even more colorful?

Why might it be helpful to chop/grate vegetables very small in a recipe?

Who do you know who would enjoy this dish? Why?

Ready In
20 min.

Serves
8

These flavorful chicken tacos are much leaner and a good choice for anyone looking to cut down on red meat.

Ingredients

3 tbsp. balsamic vinegar
2 tbsp. canned chipotle peppers in adobo sauce, *finely chopped*
3 tsp. garlic salt
4 c. cooked skinless chicken, *chopped or shredded*

4 c. shredded cabbage or prepared coleslaw mix
1 c. red onion, *finely diced*
16 (6-inch) corn tortillas
1 c. Mexican-style or Feta cheese, *crumbled*
2 avocados, *peeled, pitted, chopped*

Directions

1. In a medium bowl, mix together balsamic vinegar, chipotle peppers, and garlic salt. Add in chicken, cabbage, and onion, mix well.

2. To warm tortillas, heat in a hot skillet for 1 minute on each side. Or place tortillas on a large plate and top with a damp paper towel. Microwave on high for 2 minutes or until tortillas are warm.

3. Spoon filling into warm tortillas and top with cheese and avocado. Serve immediately.

✳ *Tip: You can substitute jarred salsa if you can't find canned chipotle peppers in adobo.*

Nutrition Info *per 2-taco serving*

Total calories: 340
Carbohydrates: 32 g
Total fat: 12 g
Saturated fat: 4 g
Protein: 27 g
Fiber: 7 g
Sodium: 360 mg

 Why do you think fast food often contains more fat, salt, and sugar than homemade?

What are some advantages and disadvantages of fast food? How about homemade food?

CORN AND BLACK BEAN SALAD

Ready In
10 min.

Serves
4

Canned beans make a terrific addition to salads. They're an inexpensive way to add protein to a meal and require little preparation. This salad features black beans and a mix of colorful vegetables, so it has lots of fiber to keep you full. It can be eaten as a side or as a complete meatless meal. Chop the vegetables very small and it also makes a great salsa.

Ingredients

2 tbsp. extra-virgin olive oil	½ c. tomato, *chopped*
Red wine vinegar, *to taste*	½ c. red onion, *chopped*
Fresh lime juice, *to taste*	1 tsp. cumin
½ c. canned black beans, *drained and rinsed*	1 tsp. chili pepper
½ c. fresh, defrosted, or canned corn kernels	½ tsp. salt
½ c. red or green bell peppers, *chopped*	½ tsp. pepper

Directions

1. Mix together beans and vegetables in a large bowl.

2. Toss with olive oil, vinegar, and lime juice.

Nutrition Info *per ½ cup serving*

Total calories: 122
Carbohydrates: 13 g
Total fat: 7 g
Saturated fat: 1 g
Protein: 3 g
Fiber: 3.5 g
Sodium: 186 mg

Which flavors stick out when you eat this recipe? Which ingredients "blend in?"

What are some fun additions or changes you can make to this recipe?

How could you turn this into a main dish?

Ready In 30 min.   **Serves** 4

It's easy to find burritos in the frozen foods case at your grocery store or at fast food restaurants. But you can make your own with a lot more flavor and nutrients. These egg burritos can be frozen and reheated for breakfast, dinner, or any time you need a balanced meal on the go.

Ingredients

3 green onions, *sliced*	4 large eggs
1 red or green bell pepper, *diced small*	¼ c. cilantro, *chopped* (optional)
1 clove garlic, *minced*	¾ tsp. ground cumin, *divided*
1 (15.5-oz) can no-salt added black beans, *drained and rinsed*	¼ tsp. ground black pepper
	4 (8-inch) whole wheat flour tortillas
2 tsp. oil, *divided*	½ c. low-fat cheddar cheese, *grated*

※ **Notes:** *If you double the recipe, do not double cumin. Also, when a recipe says "divided" or "separated," it means you will use that ingredient in more than one place in the dish, rather than all at once.*

Directions

1. Heat oil in a medium skillet over medium heat. Add beans, green onions, bell pepper, and garlic. Cook until peppers are soft, about 3 minutes. Add ½ tsp. ground cumin and black pepper. Transfer mixture to a bowl.

2. In a small bowl, crack eggs. Add remaining ¼ tsp. cumin. Beat mixture lightly with a fork.

3. Wipe out skillet with a paper towel. Heat 1 tsp oil on medium-low. Add egg mixture. Cook, stirring occasionally, until eggs are as firm as you like. If using cilantro, add now.

4. Spoon egg mixture into the center of each tortilla, dividing evenly. Add beans and veggies. Sprinkle cheese on top.

5. Fold tortilla over mixture and serve.

※ **Tips:** *Burritos can be frozen for up to one week. Wrap tightly in plastic wrap, cover with aluminum foil, and freeze. To reheat, remove foil and plastic. Microwave 1 ½ - 2 minutes, turning as needed. Or, remove plastic wrap and re-cover in aluminum foil. Heat in a toaster oven or regular oven at 300° F for about 6 minutes.*

Nutrition Info *per burrito*

Total calories: 350	**Total fat:** 9 g	**Protein:** 20 g	**Sodium:** 510 mg
Carbohydrates: 45 g	**Saturated fat:** 1 g	**Fiber:** 9 g	

How might this recipe be more nutritious than a frozen burrito?

If you didn't have enough money for all of the ingredients, what would you leave out?

Ready In 25 min. | **Serves** 6

Fish tacos are a specialty from Baja California, Mexico. Fish and shellfish are a great source of protein and nutrients such as healthy fats. Most seafood can be found frozen and is sometimes less expensive than fresh, but just as healthy.

Ingredients

1 pound white fish fillets, such as cod, *cut into 1-inch pieces*
1 tbsp. olive oil
2 tbsp. lemon juice
1 tbsp. taco seasoning
12 (6-inch) corn tortillas, *warmed*

2 c. red or green cabbage, *shredded*
2 c. tomatoes, *chopped*
½ c. plain Greek yogurt or low-fat sour cream
Hot sauce, *to taste*
Lime wedges for serving (optional)

Directions

1. Heat a large skillet.

2. In a medium bowl, combine fish, olive oil, lemon juice, and taco seasoning.

3. Add to skillet and cook, stirring constantly, over medium-high heat for 4 to 5 minutes or until fish flakes easily when tested with a fork.

4. Fill tortillas with fish mixture.

5. Top with cabbage, tomato, Greek yogurt, and hot sauce. Serve with lime wedge for squeezing over, if desired.

✳ *Tip: You can make your own flavorful taco seasoning by mixing up powdered chili, garlic, onion, cumin, paprika, dried oregano, and salt.*

Nutrition Info *per 2-taco serving*

Total calories: 239
Carbohydrates: 32 g
Total fat: 5 g
Saturated fat: 1 g
Protein: 19 g
Fiber: 4 g
Sodium: 247 mg

 Do you know anyone who doesn't eat fish? Do you think they would try this dish?

What might you make to go along with these tacos?

Ready In
10 min.

Serves
4

Are there any snacks that fill you up without weighing you down? Raw fruits and vegetables are an ideal way to refuel between meals; they're nutritious and filling without ruining your appetite. However, you may find them boring on their own. If so, try dressing up raw vegetables with a simple dip, such as the one in this recipe.

Ingredients

½ c. plain Greek yogurt or low-fat sour cream
⅓ c. prepared salsa
3 tbsp. green onions, *chopped*
½ tsp. garlic salt

1 red bell pepper, *cut into strips*
2 celery stalks, *cut into sticks*
1 c. baby carrots

Directions

1. Put sour cream, salsa, green onions, and garlic salt in a small bowl. Stir well.

2. Serve red bell pepper strips, celery sticks, and baby carrots with dip.

Nutrition Info *per 1 cup serving*

Total calories: 66
Carbohydrates: 12 g
Total fat: <1 g
Saturated fat: <1 g
Protein: 2 g
Fiber: 4.2 g
Sodium: 240 mg

 What are some other ways to add flavor to raw fruits and vegetables?

Think of your favorite raw vegetable. How could you prepare/store it for easy snacking?

FRUIT CRISP

Oats, spices, fruit baked with a touch of sugar are an easy dessert to make for your friends or family. The best part is that the fiber from the oats, fruit, and nuts (if using) slow down the absorption of the sugar, so you don't get a sugar rush or crash like other desserts. Top this with a little yogurt to make it special.

Ingredients

- 4 c. fruit, *diced or sliced*
- 4 tbsp. soft butter or oil
- 4 tbsp. brown sugar
- 8 tbsp. rolled oats
- 4 tbsp. whole wheat flour
- 1 tsp. ground cinnamon
- 6 tbsp. walnuts, pecans, or almonds, *chopped (optional)*

Microwave Directions

1. Place fruit in a microwave-safe dish.
2. Use a dish that is wide enough so that the fruit is about 1 inch deep in the bottom. Combine remaining ingredients to make oat topping and sprinkle it over the fruit.
3. Microwave on high 1-5 minutes or until fruit is as tender as you like it.

Oven Directions

1. Place fruit in the bottom of a baking dish.
2. In a separate bowl, mix together butter/oil, oats, brown sugar, flour, cinnamon, and nuts.
3. Sprinkle the mixture over the fruit.
4. Bake at 375° F for 45 minutes or until the top is golden brown.

❋ *Tip: Frozen fruit works well in this recipe. Just be sure to thaw it before using. Or you can use canned fruit that has been rinsed to remove the sugar.*

Nutrition Info *per 1 cup serving*

Total calories: 336
Carbohydrates: 48 g
Total fat: 15 g
Saturated fat: 1 g
Protein: 5 g
Fiber: 6 g
Sodium: 6 mg

Have you ever made dessert in the microwave?

What type of fruit do you think would work best in this recipe?

Ready In 15 min.   **Serves** 4

Fresh fruit, when eaten in season, is often sweet enough to make a satisfying dessert. If you like to dress it up however, this recipe for fresh fruit with a chocolate drizzle still has far less added sugar than processed candies, pastries, or ice cream.

Ingredients

2   tbsp. semi-sweet chocolate chips
2   large bananas, *peeled and cut into quarters*
8   large strawberries

¼   c. unsalted toasted coconut or chopped nuts (optional)

Directions

1. Place chocolate chips in a small microwave safe bowl. Heat on high for 10 seconds and stir. Repeat until chocolate is melted, about 30 seconds.

2. Place fruit on a small tray covered with a piece of waxed paper. Use a spoon to drizzle the melted chocolate on top of the fruit.

3. Sprinkle the fruit with chopped coconut or nuts.

4. Cover the fruit and place in the refrigerator for 10 minutes or until the chocolate hardens. Serve chilled.

Nutrition Info *per 4-piece serving*

Total calories: 112
Carbohydrates: 25 g
Total fat: 2 g
Saturated fat: 1 g
Protein: 1.6 g
Fiber: 4.7 g
Sodium: 238 mg

 What are foods with natural sugars? How can you identify foods with added sugars?

What other fruit would you use in this recipe?

© 2017 Lean's Pantry | Around the Table

GREEN SMOOTHIE

Ready In 5 min. **Serves** 2

In recent years, bottled juices and smoothies have become more popular. These can be expensive though, and often contain just as much sugar as soft drinks! This smoothie is an inexpensive, nutrient-packed alternative you can make yourself. It's also a great way to add greens to your diet, even if you don't love their flavor. Use at least one kind of frozen fruit to make this cold, thick and creamy.

Ingredients

2   large handful raw greens such as spinach or kale (about 1 c.)

1   medium banana

2   c. other fresh or frozen fruit, *chopped*

2   c. milk or milk substitute

Directions

1. Place all ingredients in a blender in the order listed.

2. Blend until smooth and creamy. Add a little water if desired for a thinner smoothie.

3. Serve immediately.

❋ *Tip: Yellow, green, or orange fruits make this smoothie a pretty color while reds and purples might make it look a little darker or grayer. Regardless, any color fruit tastes delicious!*

Nutrition Info *per 2 cup serving*

Total calories: 218
Carbohydrates: 45 g
Total fat: 1.5 g
Saturated fat: <1 g
Protein: 10 g
Fiber: 6 g
Sodium: 129 mg

 What fruits would you use for a very sweet flavor? A more tart flavor?

What could you add to make this even more nutritious?

What are the pros and cons of smoothies?

Fresh vegetables, as well as many other plant foods, have protein; in fact, calorie for calorie, some have as much protein as meat! Vegetables also contain fiber and vitamins you won't find in meat. Use whatever vegetables you like to make these savory pancakes—even leftovers from another recipe!

Ingredients

2	large eggs
½	tsp. salt
¾	c. all-purpose flour
½	c. ice water
1½	c. mixed vegetables such as zucchini, broccoli, bell peppers, green beans, or asparagus, *chopped very small*
2	green onions (scallions), *cut into 1-inch pieces*

Dipping Sauce:

2	tbsp. rice wine vinegar
2	tbsp. low-sodium soy sauce
1	tsp. sugar
	Pinch of red chile flakes, *or to taste*
2	tsp. vegetable oil

Directions

1. In a medium bowl, whisk eggs and salt until frothy. Add flour and ice water. Then, stir to make a thick batter. Gently stir in vegetables and green onions.

2. In a small skillet, heat half the oil over medium heat. Spoon in half the batter to make a pancake, spreading the vegetables evenly. Cook until crisp and golden, 4 to 5 minutes per side. Repeat with remaining oil and batter.

3. In a small bowl, stir together all ingredients for the dipping sauce.

4. Cut pancakes into quarters, arrange on a platter, and serve with dipping sauce.

❋ *Tip:* Replace ½ c. of the vegetables with diced kimchi or chopped, cooked, shrimp.

Nutrition Info *per 2-piece serving*

Total calories: 165
Carbohydrates: 22 g
Total fat: 5 g
Saturated fat: 1 g
Protein: 7.3 g
Fiber: 1.7 g
Sodium: 465 mg

What ingredients could you add to this recipe to make it extra appealing?

When could you make or serve this dish?

What do you think the purpose of the eggs are in this recipe?

MEATBALL SOUP

Ready In 40 min.

Serves 8

This is a delicious, mild version of a traditional Mexican soup called Albondigas. You can make it spicier if you like. Pound for pound, meat is more expensive than vegetables. Too much fat from animal products can also be bad for our health. It's not necessary to become a vegetarian or vegan; however, a diet rich in plant foods will benefit our health and also save us money. Soups that include vegetables and lean meat are a great way to make nourishing, hearty, and economical meals.

Ingredients

4 c. water	2 plum tomatoes, *diced*
4 c. reduced-sodium chicken broth	½ c. fresh cilantro, *chopped*
2 lbs. ground lean turkey	1 large potato, *chopped*
¼ c. mint leaves, *finely chopped*	2 carrots, *chopped*
1 clove garlic, *minced*	1 celery stalk, *chopped*
¼ tbsp. ground black pepper	2 zucchinis or yellow squash, *chopped*

Directions

1. In a pot, over medium heat: bring water and chicken broth to a boil.

2. While the liquids come to a boil, mix ground turkey, mint, garlic, pepper, and chopped tomato.

3. Roll the mixture into little balls, about 1-1½ inch diameter.

4. Once the liquids are boiling, add meatballs and cilantro. Lower heat and cook covered for 10 minutes.

5. When meatballs rise to the top, add potatoes, carrots, and celery. Continue to cook covered.

6. Once the vegetables are soft, add the zucchini and let it cook for 10 more minutes or until zucchini is tender before serving.

✻ **Tip:** *For added flavor, add lime juice, chopped chile pepper, or chopped onion to your bowl.*

Nutrition Info *per 1½ cup serving*

Total calories: 203
Carbohydrates: 5 g
Total fat: 10 g
Saturated fat: 3 g
Protein: 18 g
Fiber: 2 g
Sodium: 348 mg

 What other meat and vegetable combinations could you turn into a soup?

What grain might you add to this soup?

Have you ever made soup from scratch before?

Ready In 20 min. **Serves** 4

Very colorful foods are often more appealing to the eye than foods that are only one color. Eating a variety of colorful fruits and vegetables every day also helps to ensure you're getting the different vitamins you need. This colorful stir-fry is an Americanized version of a Chinese dish. It is usually eaten in a flour wrap, similar to a flour tortilla but you can also have it over rice.

Ingredients

2	tbsp. vegetable oil		1	red bell pepper, *very thinly sliced*
1	piece (about 1-inch) fresh ginger, *peeled then grated or minced*		3	medium carrots, *coarsely shredded* (about 2 c.)
3	cloves garlic, *minced*		1	tbsp. soy sauce
1	tbsp. toasted sesame oil		1	tbsp. cornstarch
1	small cabbage, preferably Napa or Savoy, *very thinly sliced* (about 5-6 c.)		¾	c. cold water
			2	c. cooked rice or 4 warmed flour tortillas, preferably whole grain

Directions

1. In a large skillet, heat oil on medium-high heat. Add ginger and garlic and stir-fry for a few seconds.

2. Add the sesame oil, onion, and cabbage and stir-fry for two minutes. Add the peppers and carrots. Stir-fry for a little longer.

3. Add the soy sauce and stir-fry for another minute.

4. Stir the cornstarch into the water. Add to skillet and let simmer for two minutes or until liquid is thickened and evaporated.

5. Eat the vegetables rolled up in warmed flour tortillas or over rice.

Nutrition Info *per ¼ cup serving*

Total calories: 226
Carbohydrates: 28 g
Total fat: 11 g
Saturated fat: 1 g
Protein: 6 g
Fiber: 3 g
Sodium: 543 mg
Added Sugar: <1 g

What color fruit or vegetable is hardest for you to eat enough of?

Do you know anyone who eats mostly brown or white foods? Do you think they would try these Mu Shu Vegetables?

What other vegetables might you use in this dish?

NO-COOK CHOCOLATE PUDDING

Ready In 25 min.   **Serves** 6

Have a chocolate or a sweet tooth? This is a perfect recipe to provide a little chocolatey goodness as well as some healthy fats from avocados. Cocoa powder is made from crushed cocoa beans, the same beans used to make chocolate. Cocoa beans aren't naturally sweet--the sugar is added in the chocolate making process.

Ingredients

2	ripe avocados, *peeled and cubed*
1	banana, *peeled and cubed*
¼	c. cocoa powder unsweetened
¼	c. milk or non-dairy alternatives (almond or coconut are a good choice)

2	tablespoons honey
1	teaspoon vanilla extract

Directions

1. Mix all ingredients together in a blender or food processor until creamy and smooth. Adjust texture and flavor by adding more cocoa powder or milk.

2. Spoon into individual cups if you want to be fancy. Chill in the refrigerator for 20 minutes (or eat right away if you can't wait!).

3. Top with your favorite fruit or sprinkle some toasted nuts or coconut on top.

Nutrition Info *per ½ cup serving*

Total calories: 160
Carbohydrates: 18 g
Total fat: 11 g
Saturated fat: 2 g
Protein: 3 g
Fiber: 6 g
Sodium: 64 mg
Added Sugar: 6 g

 Where does the saturated fat come from in this recipe?

Where does the sugar come from in this recipe?

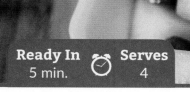

Ready In 5 min.   **Serves** 4

We often hear that it's important to drink water. A diet rich in fruits and vegetables also contains lots of water from the plants themselves. The ingredients in this salad are all hydrating. This makes it a great snack whenever you need to feel refreshed.

Ingredients

2 tsp. olive oil
2 tbsp. lime juice
⅛ tsp. salt

1 large cucumber, *diced (peel if waxed)*
1½ c. seedless red grapes, *sliced in half*
2 pears, *diced*

Directions

1. In a large bowl, whisk oil, lime juice, and salt.

2. Add grapes, cucumber, and pears and toss before serving.

✳ **Tip:** *Sprinkle with ground chile powder for a little kick.*

Nutrition Info *per 1 cup serving*

Total calories: 73
Carbohydrates: 16 g
Total fat: 2 g
Saturated fat: <1 g
Protein: <1 g
Fiber: 2 g
Sodium: 52 mg

What are some other foods that have a lot of water in them?

Why might it be helpful to get water from the foods we eat?

What else would you add to this salad to change the flavor?

PITA PIZZA

Ready In 20 min.   **Serves** 4

Pizza can be a nutritious, balanced meal if it's made with good ingredients. This pizza recipe uses whole wheat pita, which has more nutrients than white pizza dough. You add even more fiber and nutrients by putting plenty of fresh vegetables on top.

Ingredients

- 4 whole wheat pita bread
- 1 c. part-skim mozzarella cheese, *shredded*
- 1 c. low-sodium tomato or pizza sauce
- 1 c. vegetables, such as bell peppers, broccoli, mushrooms, olives, pineapple, onions, tomatoes, asparagus, and/or zucchini, *diced*

Directions

1. Preheat oven or toaster oven to 425°F. Line baking sheet with foil for easy cleanup.
2. Place the pitas on a baking sheet for assembly. Spread the tomato sauce on the pita leaving room for crust.
3. Sprinkle with cheese and add the toppings.
4. Cook pizzas in the oven for 5-8 minutes, or until cheese is melted.
5. Let cool for a minute before eating.

✳ **Tip:** *Use leftover veggies to cut down on prep time. Sprinkle with dried oregano, basil or chili flakes for even more flavor.*

Nutrition Info *per pita*

Total calories: 213
Carbohydrates: 32 g
Total fat: 6 g
Saturated fat: 3 g
Protein: 13 g
Fiber: 6 g
Sodium: 460 mg

 How many food groups does this pizza have?

How would you change this recipe if you made it at home?

What other foods can be balanced— or not— depending on how you make them?

Did you know that popcorn is a whole grain? It's also easier and less expensive to make on the stove! Sprinkle your favorite seasoning on top for a nutritious snack. Make sure your kernels are fresh for the fluffiest popcorn.

Ready In 10 min.   **Serves** 5

Ingredients

½ c. popcorn kernels
2 tbsp. oil
½ tsp. salt

Assorted toppings, such as paprika, cayenne pepper, nutritional yeast, Parmesan cheese, dried herbs

Directions

1. Add vegetable oil to a large saucepan with a lid.

2. Add popcorn kernels, cover, and heat on medium. You will hear the kernels begin to pop after a few minutes.

3. Shake the pan frequently, holding the lid in place, to make sure all the kernels cook evenly without burning.

4. When you hear the popping slow down, remove from heat. Carefully open the lid.

5. Pour into a serving bowl and add desired toppings.

Nutrition Info *per 3 cup serving*

Total calories: 135
Carbohydrates: 18 g
Total fat: 6 g
Saturated fat: <1 g
Protein: 3 g
Fiber: 3 g
Sodium: 200 mg

 Do you like the seasoning used in this recipe? What other seasoning might you try instead?

Have you ever made popcorn on the stove? Was it easier or harder than you expected?

SALSA FRESCA

Ready In 15 min.　**Serves** 4

Homemade salsa can brighten up any meal. But did you know that salsa can be made with other fruits and vegetables besides tomatoes? Try mango, peach, watermelon, pears, corn, or cucumbers for a fun and delicious twist.

Ingredients

4　stems fresh cilantro, *chopped (stems included)*
1　small red onion, *chopped*
1　medium green bell pepper, *chopped*
Hot sauce or fresh hot peppers, *to taste* (optional)
6　plum tomatoes

2　tbsp. red wine vinegar
1　lime, *juiced*
1　tbsp. ground cumin
1　tsp. olive oil
Salt, *to taste*

Directions

1. Roughly chop the cilantro. Cut the onion and peppers into large pieces. Process in a blender until coarsely chopped.

2. Quarter the tomatoes. Add, along with remaining ingredients and pulse until the mixture is chopped into small pieces.

3. Serve immediately, or cover and chill for up to three days.

No-blender Directions

1. Chop everything finely with a knife.

2. Grate the tomatoes on the large holes of a grater (over a bowl so you catch the juices!).

3. Combine all the ingredients and serve immediately or cover/chill for up to three days.

Nutrition Info *per ½ cup serving*

Total calories: 58
Carbohydrates: 10 g
Total fat: 2 g
Saturated fat: <1 g
Protein: 2 g
Fiber: 3 g
Sodium: 12 mg

What are the different flavors that you can taste in this salsa?

What would you like to eat with this salsa?

What other ingredients might you add to this recipe to give it a twist?

Ready In 10 min. | **Serves** 3

Sautéing fruit brings out the banana's sweetness and creates a delicious caramel like crust. This technique can be applied to all kinds of fruit. Lower the amount of sugar if you are making with sweeter fruits. This also makes a good topping for pancakes, yogurt or oatmeal.

Ingredients

3 bananas firm but ripe	½ tsp. cinnamon, *or adjust to taste*
1 tsp. unsalted butter	1½ tsp. fresh squeezed lemon juice
1½ tbsp brown sugar	

Directions

1. Peel bananas and cut in quarters, first by cutting in half widthwise then lengthwise.
2. In a skillet, over low heat: add butter, brown sugar and cinnamon; stir until bubbly.
3. Add banana quarters, cut side down; sauté 1-2 minutes or until golden brown.
4. Turn over and sauté the other side, until golden brown.
5. Sprinkle with the lemon juice.
6. Serve warm; drizzle pan juice over bananas.

Nutrition Info *per banana*

Total calories: 157
Carbohydrates: 37 g
Total fat: 4 g
Saturated fat: 2 g
Protein: 1 g
Fiber: 3 g
Sodium: 6 mg

What purpose do you think the lemon juice serves in this recipe?

What are some things that you can do with ripe or overripe bananas?

SESAME CHICKEN STIR-FRY

Ready In 25 min. | **Serves** 4

Restaurant meals often have far more salt, fat, and sugar than you would use at home. This Sesame Chicken with vegetables does have a little sugar for sweetness, but it also gets a lot of sweetness from fresh bell pepper and snow peas.

Ingredients

2 tsp. oil	2 tbsp. water
1 lb. boneless, skinless chicken, *cut into strips*	1½ tsp packed brown sugar
2 c. snow peas or snap peas, *trimmed*	¼ tsp. ground ginger
1 medium red bell pepper, *chopped*	1 tbsp. toasted sesame seeds
1 medium green bell pepper, *chopped*	2 green onions, *sliced*
3 tbsp. low-sodium soy sauce	2 c. cooked brown rice

Directions

1. Heat oil in large skillet. Add chicken; cook and stir-fry for 5-8 minutes or until chicken is fully cooked. Add snow peas and bell peppers; stir fry for 3 to 4 minutes more until vegetables are crisp-tender.

2. In a small bowl, combine soy sauce, water, brown sugar, and ginger; add to skillet. Cook for 3-5 minutes over medium-high heat.

3. Sprinkle with sesame seeds and green onions. Serve over brown rice.

Nutrition Info *per 1¼ cup serving*

Total calories: 313
Carbohydrates: 28 g
Total fat: 7 g
Saturated fat: 1 g
Protein: 30 g
Fiber: 5 g
Sodium: 470 mg

 Which flavors stand out in this recipe?

If you could replace one ingredient in this recipe with a different one, what would it be?

What other vegetables would taste good in this dish?

Ready In 40 min.   **Serves** 8

Choosing extra lean or lean ground meat keeps this recipe heart healthy. If you want to make it vegetarian, substitute chopped mushrooms. This sauce is great to keep in the freezer for a last minute meal.

Ingredients

2 tsp. olive oil	2 cloves garlic, *finely chopped*
1 pound lean ground turkey or beef	1 tsp. dried oregano
2 (14½-ounce) cans diced tomatoes, *juice reserved*	1 tsp. ground black pepper
1 green bell pepper, *finely chopped*	1 pound pasta, preferably whole wheat
1 medium onion, *finely chopped*	

Directions

1. Heat olive oil in a medium pot over medium heat.

2. Add turkey and cook, stirring occasionally for 5 to 10 minutes or until cooked through. Drain fat.

3. Stir in tomatoes with their juice, bell pepper, onion, garlic, oregano, and ground black pepper. Bring to a boil and reduce heat. Cover and simmer for 15-20 minutes, stirring occasionally.

4. Meanwhile, cook pasta according to package directions; drain well.

5. Serve sauce over spaghetti.

Nutrition Info *per 1½ cup serving*

Total calories: 357
Carbohydrates: 53 g
Total fat: 7 g
Saturated fat: 2 g
Protein: 21 g
Fiber: 4 g
Sodium: 272 mg

 What does "balanced diet" mean to you?

Think of a time when you did not eat a balanced diet. How did you feel?

SPICED TRAIL MIX

Ready In 10 min.   **Serves** 12

In order to keep them low-cost and last long on the shelf, processed snack foods often contain preservatives or other ingredients you would never use at home. These ingredients may also negatively your health. Mix up a batch of this trail mix to pack as a snack. Just a little bit is enough to satisfy cravings for sweet, salt, and crunch without a lot of junk.

Ingredients

1   c. peanuts or other nuts
1   c. raisins or other dried fruit
1   c. sunflower or pumpkin seeds, *raw or roasted*
1   c. bite-sized pretzels, dry low sugar cereal, or small crackers

1   tbsp. paprika and/or cinnamon
Salt, *to taste*
1   c. dried shredded coconut, chocolate chips, or additional dried fruit (optional)

Directions

1.   Toss all ingredients well and enjoy.

✳   *Tip: Look for cereals with less than 6g of sugar per serving.*

Nutrition Info *per ¼ cup serving*

Total calories: 196
Carbohydrates: 19 g
Total fat: 13 g
Saturated fat: 2 g
Protein: 6 g
Fiber: 4 g
Sodium: 113 mg

 What other ingredients might you use or substitute in this recipe?

Do you like the seasoning used in this recipe? What other seasoning might you try instead?

How might a snack like this come in handy in your life?

Ready In 15 min.   **Serves** 4

If you have a sweet tooth, try adding naturally sweet ingredients to healthy dishes to satisfy your cravings. This salad gets plenty of sweetness from fresh orange segments and dried cranberries, as well from a dressing made with orange juice. Sliced nuts give it a satisfying crunch.

Ingredients

3   c. baby spinach leaves, *washed*
3   oranges, *peeled and broken into sections or sliced*
3   tbsp. sliced almonds
¼   c. dried cranberries

1   tbsp. olive oil
3   tbsp. orange juice, *squeezed from 1 orange*
2   tbsp. rice vinegar

Directions

1. In a serving bowl, combine spinach, oranges, and cranberries.

2. In a bowl, whisk together olive oil, orange juice, and rice vinegar for the dressing.

3. Toss salad with dressing. Sprinkle with almonds and serve.

Nutrition Info *per 1 cup serving*

Total calories: 150
Carbohydrates: 21 g
Total fat: 4 g
Saturated fat: <1 g
Protein: 3 g
Fiber: 4 g
Sodium: 20 mg

What could you substitute for oranges and cranberries if they weren't available?

How does your body feel after eating a salad like this?

Do you like having a "crunch" added to your salads or dishes? What are other ingredients that you may use to do this?

SPRING SPREAD

Think back on everything you've eaten in the last two days—what colors of the rainbow have you eaten a lot of? Which have you missed? Eating a rainbow of fruits and vegetables every day increases your chance of getting the variety of vitamins and minerals you need. This easy cream cheese spread includes four rainbow colors and can be kept refrigerated for several days. It's also lighter and more flavorful than plain cream cheese.

Ingredients

4	oz. low-fat cream cheese, *whipped or softened*
½	carrot, *grated*
½	red bell pepper, *finely diced*
2	green onions, *finely chopped*
1	tbsp. fresh herbs, *chopped* (see tip)
1	tsp. freshly squeezed lemon or lime juice

Serve with: whole grain crackers, tortillas, bagels, celery sticks, or cucumber slices

Directions

1. Mix all ingredients with a rubber spatula until creamy.

2. Use as a spread for breads, crackers, or on vegetables.

❋ *Tip: This is a great way to use up leftover herbs (such as dill, thyme, oregano, basil) and vegetables.*

Nutrition Info *per 2 tbsp. serving*

Total calories: 61
Carbohydrates: 3 g
Total fat: 4 g
Saturated fat: 3 g
Protein: 2 g
Fiber: <1 g
Sodium: 106 mg

 What could you add to make this have even more colors of the rainbow?

Which colors of rainbow do you tend to eat the least of? The most of?

When would you make or eat this spread? (breakfast, snack, bring to a party, etc.)

Ready In 45 min. | **Serves** 6

It's not necessary for most of us to eat meat at every meal, or even every day. Protein builds bones, muscles, cartilage, skin, and blood, but it can be found in foods other than meat. To make a satisfying vegetarian entrée, choose a recipe with plenty of fresh vegetables, whole grains, beans, and/or legumes.

Ingredients

1 tbsp. vegetable oil
1 onion, *diced*
2 cloves garlic, *finely chopped*
2 zucchini or yellow summer squash, *diced* (fresh or frozen)
1 c. corn fresh, canned, or frozen
2 bell peppers, *diced*
½ tsp. black pepper
½ tsp. salt
1 tbsp. chili powder

1 tsp. ground cumin
1 (16-oz.) can low-sodium pinto beans, *drained and rinsed*
1 (16-oz.) can low-sodium black beans, *drained and rinsed*
1 (16-oz.) can low-sodium red kidney beans, *drained and rinsed*
2 (15-oz.) cans low-sodium diced tomatoes
1 tbsp. molasses (optional)

Directions

1. In a stockpot, heat vegetable oil over medium heat. Add onion and garlic then cook until soft, about 2 minutes. Add zucchini or squash, corn, and bell peppers then cook until soft, about 5 minutes. Stir in remaining ingredients and bring to a boil.

2. Reduce heat, cover, and simmer for 20 to 25 minutes, stirring occasionally.

3. Serve immediately or cool completely then store in the refrigerator or freezer.

Nutrition Info *per 1 cup serving*

Total calories: 370
Carbohydrates: 66 g
Total fat: 5 g
Saturated fat: 1 g
Protein: 20 g
Fiber: 19 g
Sodium: 580 mg

 What are some other ways to add beans to your diet?

If you made this for your friends, would they miss having meat? Why or why not?

TURKEY APPLE SAUSAGE MUFFIN SANDWICHES

Ready In 30 min. | **Serves** 6

Fast food meals can be loaded with salt, fat, and sugar. They may taste good, but they leave us feeling weighed down. These homemade turkey sausage sandwiches have plenty of the protein and fiber that we need without the extra processed ingredients. They're not just for breakfast.

Ingredients

Turkey Apple Sausage:
1   pound lean ground turkey
1   red apple, *cored and finely chopped*
2   garlic cloves, *minced and divided*
½   tsp. dried thyme
¼   tsp. red pepper flakes
1   tsp. dried sage
¼   tsp. ground black pepper
⅛   tsp. ground coriander
2   tsp. oil

Breakfast Sandwich:
2   c. mushrooms, *chopped*
1   medium onion, *chopped*
6   whole wheat English muffins
6   slices tomato

Directions

1. In a large bowl, combine turkey, apple, one garlic clove, thyme, red pepper flakes, sage, ground black pepper, and coriander; mix well.

2. Form the turkey mixture into 6 patties.

3. Heat 1 tsp. oil in skillet over medium heat.

4. Cook patties until they are cooked through, about 5 to 7 minutes per side. Set aside.

5. Heat 1 tsp. oil in skillet over medium heat.

6. Add mushrooms, onions, and garlic. Sauté until the mushrooms are tender and onions begin to brown, about 5 minutes.

7. Cut each English muffin in half. Place a Turkey Apple Sausage patty, ⅙th of mushroom-onion mixture, and a slice of tomato on 6 English muffin halves.

8. Cover each sandwich with the other English muffin half and enjoy!

Nutrition Info *per muffin*

Total calories: 269   **Total fat:** 6 g   **Protein:** 19 g   **Sodium:** 459 mg
Carbohydrates: 35 g   **Saturated fat:** 1 g   **Fiber:** ? g

How are these different in flavor, texture, and color than a fast food sandwich?

What ingredients would you add to this recipe? Take away?

What benefits do you think there are to using a whole wheat English muffin as opposed to a regular one?

Ready In 30 min. **Serves** 4

To eat a balanced diet, it's not necessary to make several different dishes at each meal. Many easy, filling one-pot recipes include everything you need for a balanced meal. This recipe for "un-fried" rice is lower in fat and sodium than restaurant fried rice, and it contains at least three of the five food groups. This recipe comes out best with leftover rather than freshly cooked rice.

Ingredients

- 1   tbsp. oil
- 1   clove garlic, *minced*
- 2   c. diced raw vegetables such as onion, celery, bell pepper, cabbage, broccoli, green beans, peas, zucchini, mushrooms, or bean sprouts
- 1   egg, *beaten*

- 2   c. cooked rice cold, preferably brown rice
- 2   tbsp. soy sauce
- Black pepper to taste
- 1   c. cooked chicken or shrimp (optional)
- 1   c. mango or pineapple, *chopped* (optional)

Directions

1. Heat oil until sizzling in the bottom of large skillet.

2. Stir-fry garlic and vegetables so they are cooked but still a little crisp.

3. Add shrimp or chicken to the skillet, if using, and cook for 2 minutes.

4. Push everything to one side. Add the egg directly into the exposed bottom of the pan and scramble

5. Add rice, soy sauce, black pepper, and other optional ingredients. Turn heat down to medium-low. Cook until heated through, stirring frequently.

Nutrition Info *per 1 cup serving*

Total calories: 322
Carbohydrates: 50 g
Total fat: 9 g
Saturated fat: 1 g
Protein: 12 g
Fiber: 6 g
Sodium: 794 mg

 How would you personalize this recipe to make it unique?

What do you think of adding the optional mango or pineapple to this dish? Do you often prepare "sweet and salty" meals?

VEGETABLE NOODLE BOWL

Ready In 20 min.

Serves 8

Whole grain breads and pastas are often more filling than ones made from white flours because they have more fiber and healthy fats. They may also keep their texture longer without getting soggy. This recipe calls for whole wheat noodles. The longer the noodles sit, the more they absorb the seasonings in the recipe. Their hearty texture, when combined with crunchy vegetables, really gives you something to chew on!

Ingredients

1   pound whole wheat spaghetti (or any Asian noodles, like soba)
3   tbsp. low-sodium soy sauce
4   tsp. toasted sesame oil
1   tsp. hot chili sauce (like Sriracha), *to taste*
2   garlic cloves, *finely minced or grated*
1   bunch scallions, *chopped* (about 1 c.)

1   cucumber, *cut in half lengthwise and thinly chopped* (about 1 c.)
2   carrots, *coarsely grated* (about 1 c.)
½   head of cabbage, *shredded* (about 1 c.)
Salt and pepper, *to taste*
1   c. firm tofu, *diced* (optional)

Directions

1. Prepare the noodles according to the package instructions. Rinse them under cold water and put them in a strainer to drain.

2. In a large bowl, mix the soy sauce, sesame oil, chili sauce, scallions, garlic, cucumber, carrot, and cabbage. Add the noodles toss everything together with a fork or tongs. Gently stir in tofu, if using. Taste and add salt and pepper as needed.

3. Let the noodles sit in the fridge for about an hour, if you can, before serving. The flavors will mingle and become more intense.

Nutrition Info *per 2 cup serving*

Total calories: 237
Carbohydrates: 45 g
Total fat: 4 g
Saturated fat: 1 g
Protein: 9 g
Fiber: 6 g
Sodium: 238 mg

 Which do you think is more satisfying to eat— food with chewy or crunchy texture, or soft, mushy foods? Why?

What other ingredients would you use in this recipe at home? (vegetables, proteins, seasonings)

Can you taste the whole wheat noodles in the recipe, or does the flavor blend in?

Ready In 60 min. **Serves** 4

Brown rice is a good alternative to white rice as it includes fiber, which helps to keep everything moving through our bodies. The bran content is also rich in B-complex vitamins and minerals, which helps to keep us energized throughout the day.

Ingredients

1	c. short grain brown rice
2	c. water
3	tbsp. rice vinegar
1	tsp. sugar
1	cup baby spinach leaves or alfalfa sprouts
1	cucumber

1	carrot
1	avocado
4	sheets nori (dried seaweed)
	Sesame seeds for garnish (optional)
	Low-sodium soy sauce for dipping

Directions

1. Rinse and drain brown rice, place into a saucepan over medium heat, and pour in water. Bring to a boil, and simmer until rice has absorbed the water, about 45 minutes. Add rice vinegar and sugar to cooked brown rice. Mix well and set aside.

2. Cut carrot and cucumber into 8 long thin strips, each. Cut seeds off cucumber strips.

3. Cut avocado into half, remove skin and pit, and cut each half into 8 slices.

4. Place nori sheet horizontally in front of you. Spread rice evenly on 2/3 of nori sheet; lay a few leaves of spinach or a small amount of sprouts in the bottom third of the rice. Place 2 cucumber strips, 2 carrot strips, and 4 pieces avocado on top. (*One possible layout is shown right.*)

5. Slightly dampen the top edge of the nori. Starting from the bottom, roll up tightly. Press the damp edge to seal.

6. Cut into thick pieces and sprinkle with sesame seeds, if desired. Enjoy with or without soy sauce on the side.

※ *Tip: Three cups leftover cooked rice can be used in this recipe. Slightly warm it before adding the vinegar and sugar. Make sure your hands are dry before rolling your sushi.*

Nutrition Info *per rolling*

Total calories: 279	**Total fat:** 9 g	**Protein:** 6 g	**Sodium:** 47 mg
Carbohydrates: 50 g	**Saturated fat:** 1 g	**Fiber:** 6 g	

Is making sushi easier or harder than you expected?

Can you invent another sushi roll combination?

VEGGIE SCRAMBLE

Ready In 7 min. **Serves** 4

Many of us are too rushed in the morning to cook a big breakfast. We may end up eating sugary processed food, fast food, or nothing at all! This can affect our moods and energy throughout the day. Fortunately, scrambled eggs are quick and inexpensive. When prepared with vegetables—even frozen vegetables—they are more nutritious and filling.

Ingredients

8 tsp. olive oil
8 eggs
1⅓ c. fresh or frozen veggies, *chopped* (such as spinach, kale, chard, peppers, peas, onion, summer squash, mushrooms)

Salt, *to taste*
Pepper, *to taste*

Directions

1. Sauté veggies in a medium skillet with 1 tsp. of olive oil. Place in a medium-size bowl.

2. Add 1 tsp. olive oil to skillet, add eggs and stir over medium heat.

3. When eggs are partially cooked, add sautéed veggies. Cook until eggs are just set. Add a pinch of salt, pepper, and desired toppings.

✳ **Tip:** *Serve over brown rice or in a warmed whole wheat tortilla or pita bread for a complete meal.*

Nutrition Info *per 1 cup serving*

Total calories: 225
Carbohydrates: 1 g
Total fat: 18.5 g
Saturated fat: 3 g
Protein: 13 g
Fiber: <1 g
Sodium: 150 mg

Do you think a veggie scramble could keep you full for longer than a donut or bagel? Why?

What seasonings or condiments would you use to add flavor?

Ready In 25 min. **Serves** 4

Who needs pancake mix? Making pancakes from scratch is almost as fast and cheaper. Using whole grain flours also makes it healthier and more filling. This Whole Wheat Pancake holds up to all kinds of toppings without getting mushy like white pancakes. It can also made on a stove top or in a rice cooker!

Ingredients

1	c. whole wheat flour
2	tsp. baking powder
¼	tsp. salt
1	egg
1	c. milk or non-dairy alternatives

1	tbsp. canola oil or melted butter (optional)
1	c. sliced banana, chopped apple or berries (fresh or frozen) (optional)

Oil or butter for greasing the pan

Stove Top Directions

1. Heat wide skillet over medium heat.
2. In a bowl, mix together dry ingredients.
3. In a separate bowl, whisk eggs, milk, and melted butter or oil, if using. Add to flour mixture and stir.
4. Grease the pan with a little oil or butter. Spoon ¼ c. batter into the hot skillet.
5. Once pancake is bubbling and dry around the edges, flip it.
6. Cook for about 3 minutes more, or until the center of the pancake is completely dry.
7. Repeat until the batter is finished. Top with fruit, if using, and serve.

Rice Cooker Directions

1. Grease a rice cooker with butter or oil.
2. Mix other ingredients well in a bowl.
3. Pour batter into the rice cooker.
4. Cook for 1–2 cycles, or until the cake is dry in the middle.
5. Remove dish from rice cooker and flip it onto a plate. The pancake should pop out.
6. Slice the pancake in 4 and serve with your favorite topping.

Nutrition Info *per ¼-piece serving*

Total calories: 217	**Total fat:** 7 g	**Protein:** 8 g	**Sodium:** 293 mg
Carbohydrates: 34 g	**Saturated fat:** 2 g	**Fiber:** 5 g	

What is the benefit of mixing the dry ingredients and liquid ingredients separately before combining?

Why does whole grain flour have a stronger taste than white flour?

What other toppings would taste good with this pancake?

YOGURT PARFAIT

Ready In 15 min.　**Serves** 4

Looking at labels when shopping for ingredients can make all the difference of whether a dish is healthy or not. This recipe is a good example. When made with unsweetened yogurt, fresh fruit, and lower-sugar cereal, the parfait makes a nutritious breakfast or snack. When made with sweetened yogurt and cereal however, it may contain more added sugar than a candy bar! Check "Added Sugars" on the Nutrition Facts labels to find products with few or no added sugars.

Ingredients

2　c. fresh fruit or frozen fruit, try at least two different kinds, *chopped*

2　c. unsweetened yogurt

2　tbsp. 100% fruit spread or honey

1　c. low sugar granola or low sugar dry cereal

Directions

1.　Wash and cut fruit into small pieces.

2.　In a bowl, mix the yogurt and fruit spread together.

3.　Layer each of the parfaits in four bowls, mugs, or glasses as follows: ¼ c. fruit, ¼ c. yogurt, 2 tbsp. granola (repeat one more time). Do this for all four servings.

✳ *Tip: Use a clear glass/plastic cup or jar when you make these so you can see the beautiful layers.*

Nutrition Info *per 1 cup serving*

Total calories: 272
Carbohydrates: 44 g
Total fat: 7 g
Saturated fat: 4 g
Protein: 9 g
Fiber: 4 g
Sodium: 137 mg

 What other foods do you eat often that might have added sugars?

If you are trying to reduce your sugar consumption, what might be some ways to do it?

■ _____'s _____ and _____ Oven-baked Omelette
    name someone special   *vegetable*   *another vegetable*

Serves: 6

1. Preheat the oven to 350°F.

2. In a big bowl, whisk 8 eggs with ½ cup of _____.
                                  milk or non-dairy alternative

3. Heat 2 tablespoons of butter or oil in a large oven-proof skillet over medium heat.

   Then add 1–2 cups of chopped _____.
                               your chosen vegetables

4. When the vegetables are tender, add 1 teaspoon _____.
                                  dried herbs or spices

5. Pour the egg mixture over top the other ingredients in the skillet. Allow to cook, without stirring, for 1–2 minutes.

6. Sprinkle with a handful of crumbled _____, if desired, then bake in the oven
                                  cheese

   for 15–20 minutes or until the center is just firm.

7. Remove the frittata from the oven and let cool a little before slicing and serving.

❋ *Tip: If you don't have an oven-proof skillet, oil or butter the bottom of a baking pan. Spread vegetable mixture on the bottom and pour in beaten eggs before baking.*

IDEA BANK

Vegetables	Herbs and Spices	Cheese
spinach	basil	Parmesan or Romano
squash	oregano	cheddar
mushrooms	thyme	mozzarella
Swiss chard	parsley	Swiss cheese
asparagus	tarragon	Jack cheese
peas	chile powder	
corn kernels	turmeric	
onion	cilantro	
broccoli		
bell pepper		

WRITE YOUR OWN RECIPE: CHEESY BAKED PASTA

■ Cheesy Baked _____ with _____
                        pasta   *one selected ingredient or*
                                               seasoning from the recipe

Serves: 8

1. Preheat oven to 400°F. Grease a baking dish.

2. Boil a large pot of salted water. Add 1 pound of whole grain _____
                                                                        pasta

   and cook until it's almost, but not quite, done (still a little firm, also known as *al dente*).

3. While the pasta cooks, grate 8 oz. _____ into a large bowl.
                                            cheese

   Add a cup of milk and a teaspoon of _____.
                                            herbs and spices

4. Fold in 2 cups of chopped _____ and some _____.
                                    greens   *extras*

5. If you'd like, sprinkle some _____ over the top.
                                      toppings

6. Drain the pasta and mix with the other ingredients. Then pour the whole thing into your baking dish.

   Bake 15 minutes or until golden brown on top.

IDEA BANK

Pasta
macaroni (or whole wheat
   macaroni)
spaghetti
shells
penne
rice stick noodles
egg noodles

Cheese
Parmesan
cheddar
Monterey Jack cheese
Gruyère, mozzarella, or Swiss

Herbs and Spices
dried or fresh oregano
fresh basil
fresh parsley
chile powder
garlic powder
mustard

Greens (raw or cooked)
cooked spinach
Swiss chard
kale
arugula
collards

Extras
cooked chicken, ham, or sausage
caramelized onions
sautéed mushrooms
chopped sun-dried tomatoes
chopped pitted olives
corn
frozen peas
cooked broccoli or cauliflower

Toppings
bread crumbs or croutons
crispy onions
crushed crackers or chips
more shredded cheese

■ _____'s Dinner Salad with _____ and _____
  name someone special   *salad greens*   *protein or whole grain*

Serves: 6

1. In a giant bowl, whisk together ⅓ cup olive oil with 3 tablespoons _____,
   acid

   1 teaspoon _____, and a pinch of salt.
   dried spices or herbs

2. To the bowl, add up to 2 cups each of _____, _____,
   crunchy raw vegetables   *your chosen cooked protein or whole grain*

   _____, and _____. Toss them in the dressing. Taste a piece of
   something juicy, chopped   *another fruit or vegetable*

   lettuce and adjust seasonings or acid.

3. Add about 6 cups of _____, chopped or torn in bite-sized pieces.
   your chosen salad greens

4. Add up to 1 cup of _____.
   something with texture, for fun

5. Toss everything really well to coat with the dressing. Serve at room temperature.

IDEA BANK

Acids
fresh citrus juice
apple cider
balsamic vinegar
wine vinegar
rice vinegar with a little soy
   sauce
Or try a combination!

Herbs and Spices
basil
oregano
thyme
parsley
mint
ginger
chile flakes
mustard
black pepper

Raw Vegetables
chopped bell peppers
chopped or shredded carrots
sliced avocado
sliced cucumbers
chopped celery
shaved fennel

Cooked Proteins & Whole Grains
cooked chicken, turkey, or steak
cooked shrimp
canned tuna or salmon (drained)
cubed marinated tofu
sliced hard-boiled egg
cooked whole legumes like
   chickpeas or kidney beans
cooked quinoa
cooked whole grain pasta
cooked wild rice, brown rice, or
   red rice

Something Juicy
tomatoes
corn kernels
orange or grapefruit segments
sliced plums or peaches
sliced apples or pears
chunks of mango or pineapple

Salad Greens
spinach
lettuce
cabbage
arugula
kale
Or try a combination!

Fun additions
pitted olives
nuts or seeds
crumbled or shredded salty
   cheese
sliced soft cheese
crunchy tortilla strips or croutons
dried fruit such as raisins,
   cranberries, cherries
Or try a combination!

■ Fried _____ with _____ and _____
         whole grain   *protein*   *vegetable or fruit*

Serves: 4 *(If doubling this recipe, make in batches or use two pans.)*

1. Heat a big skillet over high heat, then add 2 tablespoons vegetable oil (not olive).

2. When the oil is hot, turn down the heat to medium, and add a handful of

   chopped _____ .
           type of onion, garlic, or shallot

3. Stir in a cup of _____ .
                    your chosen protein

4. When the protein is cooked through, remove from pan and set aside. Add 1 tbsp. vegetable oil and 2

   cups chopped _____ . Keep stirring.
               vegetables, at least 2 kinds

5. Add 2 cups of cold cooked _____ , ½ cup of _____ ,
                            your chosen whole grain   *something fun (optional)*

   and a few tablespoons of _____ .
                           salty or spicy sauce

6. Stir everything until all the ingredients are heated through and steaming. Taste and adjust the season-

   ings. Serve hot.

IDEA BANK

Proteins
peeled shrimp
chopped chicken breast
chopped ham
lean ground beef or turkey
cubed tofu, tempeh, or seitan
eggs, beaten

Whole Grains
brown rice
quinoa
barley
farro
whole wheat couscous

Vegetables
celery
zucchini
carrots
peas
bell peppers
broccoli or cauliflower
scallions
mushrooms
cabbage
asparagus
green beans

Fun Additions
roasted peanuts, walnuts, or
   cashews
chopped mango or pineapple
sesame seeds

Salty or Spicy Sauces
soy sauce
teriyaki sauce
fish sauce
sweet chile sauce
hot sauce

■ _____

short, but descriptive and appealing, recipe title

Yield: 4-6 servings

Ingredients

_____

_____

_____

_____

_____

_____

_____

_____

Include at least one or two fruits and/or vegetables. Don't forget amounts and prep details (chopped, cooked, etc.).

Add whole grains, protein foods, dairy, or all three.

Remember the seasonings, salt, herbs, spices, or sauces.

Directions

1. First, _____

_____

2. Next, _____

_____

If the recipe is cooked, give instructions for heating the stove, oven, or other appliance.

Remember to describe what equipment to use.

How will people know when each step is complete or the recipe is finished? Give sensory details.

3. Then, _____

_____

4. Finally, _____

_____

5. Serve with _____

Don't forget to _____!

Where do you find trustworthy nutrition information online?

EatFresh.org🌱 makes shopping and home cooking easy. Go to EatFresh.org🌱 right now and start exploring!

» Find healthy, inexpensive, and quick recipes, including those found in this workbook.
» Print, save, share, and text recipes to your mobile phone.
» Learn lifestyle tips to keep you healthy and feeling your best.
» Ask a registered dietitian a question about nutrition, cooking, or healthy eating.
» Save time planning and shopping with meal plans.
» Apply for CalFresh/SNAP.
» Learn basic cooking skills and how to substitute ingredients to use what you already have at home.
» View the website in English, Spanish, or Chinese.
» View nutrition information for each recipe.

There are no right or wrong answers. You may skip any questions that you do not feel comfortable answering.

Name: _____

A. How true do you feel these statements are about you personally?

(For each question, please insert √ in the best answer box.)

	Not at all true	A little true	Pretty much true	Very much true
1. I can work with someone who has different opinions than mine.				
2. I can work out my problems.				
3. I can do most things if I try.				
4. There are many things that I do well.				
5. I try to understand what other people go through.				
6. I try to understand what other people feel and think.				
7. When I need help, I find someone to talk with.				
8. I try to work out problems by talking or writing about them.				
9. I understand my moods and feelings.				
10. I understand why I do what I do.				

B. How much do you agree with the following statements?

(For each question, please insert √ in the best answer box.)

	Strongly disagree	Disagree	Somewhat disagree	Not sure	Somewhat agree	Agree	Strongly agree
1. I get satisfaction from knowing the food I eat is good for my health.							
2. Eating foods that I know are good for my body brings me comfort.							
3. I feel that nourishing my body is a meaningful activity.							
4. I eat in a way that expresses care for my body.							

C. How often do you experience or feel any of the following statements about you personally?

(For each question, please insert √ in the best answer box.)

	Never or rarely	Sometimes	Often	Usually or always
1. I eat so quickly that I don't taste what I'm eating.				
2. I notice when there are subtle flavors in the foods I eat.				
3. I snack without noticing that I am eating.				
4. I notice when the food I eat affects my emotional state.				
5. When I'm feeling stressed, I'll go find something to eat.				

D. How good are you at each of the cooking skills below?

(For each question, please insert √ in the best answer box.)

	Very poor	Poor	Somewhat poor	Not sure	Somewhat good	Good	Very good
1. Cook food on a stove or in a pot or pan							
2. Peel and chop vegetables (such as potatoes, carrots, onions, broccoli)							
3. Bake or roast food in the oven							
4. Use herbs and spices to flavor dishes							

5. Which of the cooking skills listed above would you like to learn or improve? Circle all the corresponding numbers that apply:

Cooking Skills   #1   #2   #3   #4

E. How good are you at each of the food skills below?

(For each question, please insert √ in the best answer box.)

	Very poor	Poor	Somewhat poor	Not sure	Somewhat good	Good	Very good
1. Plan meals ahead (e.g. for the day/week ahead)							
2. Plan how much food to buy							
3. Know what budget you have to spend on food							
4. Balance meals based on nutrition advice on what is healthy							
5. Shop with a grocery list							
6. Compare prices before you buy food							
7. Read the nutrition information on food labels							
8. Follow recipes when cooking							
9. Prepare or cook a healthy meal with only a few ingredients on hand							
10. Keep basic items in your pantry for putting meals together (e.g. herbs/spices, dried/canned goods)							

11. Which of the food skills listed above would you like to learn or improve? Circle all the corresponding numbers that apply:

Food Skills   #1   #2   #3   #4   #5   #6   #7   #8   #9   #10

F. Nutrition Questions

1. How many times a day do you eat fruit?
   - ❏ I rarely eat fruit
   - ❏ Less than 1 time a day (a couple of times a week)
   - ❏ 1 time a day
   - ❏ 2 times a day
   - ❏ 3 times a day
   - ❏ 4 or more times a day

2. How many times a day do you eat vegetables?
   - ❏ I rarely eat vegetables
   - ❏ Less than 1 time a day (a couple of times a week)
   - ❏ 1 time a day
   - ❏ 2 times a day
   - ❏ 3 times a day
   - ❏ 4 or more times a day

3. Yesterday, did you drink any water, such as from a glass, bottle, or a water fountain?
   - ❏ No, I didn't drink any water yesterday
   - ❏ Yes, I drank water 1 time yesterday
   - ❏ Yes, I drank water 2 times yesterday
   - ❏ Yes, I drank water 3 times yesterday
   - ❏ Yes, I drank water 4 times yesterday
   - ❏ Yes, I drank water 5 times yesterday

4. During the past 7 days how often did you drink punch, sports drinks or other fruit-flavored drinks? (Do not count 100% fruit juice or diet drinks.)
   - ❏ I did not drink punch, sports drinks, or other fruit-flavored drinks
   - ❏ 1 to 3 times during the past 7 days
   - ❏ 4 to 6 times during the past 7 days
   - ❏ 1 time per day
   - ❏ 2 times per day
   - ❏ 3 times per day
   - ❏ 4 or more times per day

5. During the past 7 days how often did you drink any regular (not diet) sodas or soft drinks?
   - ❏ I did not drink any regular (not diet) sodas
   - ❏ 1 to 3 times during the past 7 days
   - ❏ 4 to 6 times during the past 7 days
   - ❏ 1 time per day
   - ❏ 2 times per day
   - ❏ 3 times per day
   - ❏ 4 or more times per day

6. How often do you eat breakfast?
   - ❏ Never
   - ❏ Rarely (about 1 day per week)
   - ❏ Sometimes (about 2-3 days per week)
   - ❏ Often (about 4-5 days per week)
   - ❏ Usually (about 6 days per week)
   - ❏ Always (7 days per week)

7. How would you rate your eating habits? Write a number from 1 to 10: _____

Made in the USA
Middletown, DE
06 June 2022

66722573R00044